I0151462

QUIDDITY, ROGUERY, RUE: A COMPENDIUM OF LIGHT(ER) VERSE

poems by

Adam LeFevre

Finishing Line Press
Georgetown, Kentucky

QUIDDITY, ROGUERY, RUE: A COMPENDIUM OF LIGHT(ER) VERSE

—Uncloaked, he stood before the gods at last, confessing his mortality. To reward him for his honesty they granted him one wish. "I wish to be always on the side of the laugh," he said. Upon hearing this, the gods laughed.
—Soren Kierkegaard

Publisher: Leah Maines
Editor: Christen Kincaid
Cover Art: Nellie Geraghty
Author Photo: Dion Ogust
Cover Design: Elizabeth Maines McCleavy

Printed in the USA on acid-free paper.
Order online: www.finishinglinepress.com
also available on amazon.com

Author inquiries and mail orders:
Finishing Line Press
P. O. Box 1626
Georgetown, Kentucky 40324
U. S. A.

Table of Contents

QUIDDITY

—from The Big Book of Rhymes And Riddles

What use is a shovel in Heaven?
What chance has a candle in Hell?
What memory has ten of eleven?
What good is escape to a cell?

Function demands utility;
Proof, a definite place
Where quiddity is quiddity
And the mirror absorbs your face.

Belief requires more zesting
A brine of tears and prayer
Otherwise you're just investing
In shovelfuls of air.

HOW TO STALK THE TRUTH
— from "A Field Guide to Forgetting"

Always from downwind.
Always from behind.
Always with a clear escape route
Fast in mind.

THE UNHAPPY HARBOR

It's the same old story:
an unhappy harbor gets drunk
and stows away on a ship
which turns out to be the sea itself.

Whereas other stories
might usefully examine in detail
the nature of that unhappiness,
this story presumes it intrinsic,
self-explanatory, barely worth mentioning.
If you don't already know
why the harbor acted with such abandon
this probably isn't the story for you.

Though it's impossible to prevent a seafarer's dream
from intersecting the story at some point
(usually about mid-way through)
it will in no way affect its course
and will, without consequence, retreat
into the fogbank from which it so suddenly emerged.
Ignoring receding *ahoys*, the story will just plow on.

Who among us wouldn't predict the harbor
must one day reconcile with *terra firma?*
Which of us doesn't long to believe our own destiny
implies return? ·
Those of you who become queasy
when a story doesn't weigh a theme or two
by which to anchor itself in our consciousness and memory
will experience considerable *mal de mer.*
The story will go on without a harbor.
It's really very simple:
an unhappy harbor is lost
trying to discover a new story.

FIELD TRIP TO THE LIMITS OF
OUR ANCIENT MONSTERS

Here,
they stopped.
Where these columns align
marks the farthest reach
of their dreadful incisors.

They made hunger ideal.
The more they ate, the more they wanted to eat.
So why did they stop here?
The distance behind you.
didn't even exist back then.
It had been entirely eaten.

Nothing in their time
could divert
the punctuality of their teeth
nor the acuity of their tongues.
What we call the horizon was almost in their mouth
when some mysterious reckoning
stopped them in their tracks right where we're standing.

Was it the persistence of a natural law
like entropy, or nausea, a sudden distaste
that kept them from finishing off
the last few mouthfuls of this world?
Was it the sickness of self-consciousness that did them in
or some sudden random celestial mayhem?

To be honest, children, no one knows for sure.
Though we live and die by our *isms*,

this world is reticent at its core.
We don't know why we survived, not them
nor why they lost their appetite for this place,
nor what became of them.
They left no relics except our dreams.
Maybe they conceived time in a different way
and thought they were just stepping out and away
for a breather, a smoke, just for an eon or two
always planning to come back
in what would seem to them just a few minutes
to fulfill their promise
like Christ our Savior, starved to he done with it
but of course, in the case of the monsters,
without the irony or the onus of love.

A NECESSARY DIGRESSION

One day on a coffee break, without warning a friend of mine... a flower sprouted right out of the middle of his forehead! His job had always irked him. He was a fact-checker for the Department of Dreaming, a real no-win, dead-end kind of situation. I'd always advised him, "Pal, don't let the drool on your Grandsire's nether lip crystallize into memory of pearl". But even I was amazed that this remarkably predictable world of ours, albeit locked in the clutches of a humorless and despotic winter, would be so sassy and classless to play this kind of trick on him. But, that florid protuberance (aberrance or miracle, depending on your point of view) emerging from what the Hindus might call his "third eye", was no less real than the nose which had occupied his face from the very beginning. Sure, he plucked it daily. But back it would grow overnight, more vigorous than before. An aster it was. A Michaelmas daisy As you can imagine, there was a lot of snarky talk behind his back. We're all in our own peculiar way tangled in the burgeoning nebulae of our expansive cosmos. As a friend, I did my best to comfort him. "Heavier than gold," I told him "is the *idea* of gold." "Everything blue zooms through heaven with out stopping," I told him. I told him, "You're gonna be just fine, pal. You're one of us.
There are no heroes here. Just survivors and their unprecedented children."

THE MAN WHO SAW NOTHING BUT SORROW AND MADNESS

You might be surprised to learn he had a ready smile and a contagious
     laugh, deep and round.

Sometimes wore the same dirty shirt for a week, but never because he
     hadn't a clean one.

The couple who lived next door said they often heard him singing, late at
     night and early
in the morning—light-hearted ditties glossed with finger pops and silly
     syllables.

He didn't look like a man afflicted, his skin smooth, unblemished. His
     eyes, despite all
they had encountered, never fogged over with that milky wash that so
     often clouds the prospects of the aged.

He never liked small-talk, but was remarkably skilled at it. He just had a
     way with
people. In his presence they would breathe deeper and more evenly, as if
     they were home safe in bed.

Lord, he was patient! Once in a bar I observed him explaining the infield
     fly rule to an
inebriated immigrant who spoke no English, while nursing himself just
     seltzer with lime.
He used his hands and swizzle sticks and coasters. He took his sweet time.

He assumed everyone saw what he saw, and none of us had the decency
     to tell him how
over the years we had learned after weeping to walk away, while he stayed
     right there, the last of his tribe to testify to misery.

He died at a ripe old age. Smiling. Happy to go. Not to escape the horrors
     attending this
world, nor because his heart, fractured so many times over the years, ever
     needed mending (it was never less than whole). It wasn't like that.

"My Beloved knows the funniest stories," he whispered, his eyes wide open, twinkling.

"See how she beckons me? She must have a new one to tell!"

A NEW COMMITTEE

In a late statement regarding the situation
unidentified sources report
that though the facts of the situation
remain substantially the same,
the statement regarding the situation
has altered the condition of the situation
to the extent a new committee may be required
to identify changes occasioned by
the statement regarding the situation
and perhaps to recommend a suspension of statements
regarding the situation until further notice
given the history of past statements
regarding the situation becoming
chronically "fugitive" or "mum to circumstance"
or, as one source put it, "the cause of irreparable inelegance"
such as we see here.
This new committee might easily submit its report
by the year 3630 or even before,
if every actionable case has been exhausted or satisfied,
and the most provocative silences digested;
that is, until they have nourished us.

MORNING ROUTINE

Each morning from the fog
of my shaving mirror, a hand
reaches out and touches my face.
It is the Other, wanting from me
the why and where
of his Otherness.

I go about my business,
a solid man in the community,
ten years on the zoning board,
Little League coach, etc.
Faithful husband. Indentured to rectitude.
This is the way it is.

Each morning, the hand on my face.
Each morning, I turn away.
You must choose carefully
with whom to make exchange,
with whose breath to mix
the mists of your own.

Otherwise monstrous off-spring,
conceived in a haze of reckless faith,
and nourished by your denials
will fill your house with differences
demanding your embrace.

HARD SCIENCE

In the mirror's odd remove
I wait for my reflection
To make the first move

Truth
Must be reproved
At every turn

To ascertain
If it's sacred,
Or profane

RESURRECTION, THE PAPERWORK

Nobody likes to talk about it but
After the drama of a death,
There are shit-loads of paperwork.

Certificates, notices,
Cancellations, writs.
Liens on legacies, invoices for crypts.

Imagine then, after the Resurrection,
The blank expressions on the faces
Of the scribes and legatees
When they got word of the Ascension
Having already dotted the *i*'s and crossed the *t*'s,
Sealed and signed off on the rabble-rousing rabbi's
Very public demise.

Without protocols for miracles how could they register the event?
How document as fact such a fishy disappearing act?
How explicate the Trinity and file it all in triplicate?

Death, we know, is mankind's common fate.
But all belief is open to debate.

Blessed be the scribe who can
In good conscience and with grace purport
When John Doe dies he's dead in fact
Yet not, perhaps, beyond all remedy.

The soul survives on comedy,
Where there's morning after mourning.

POSTCARD FROM PRAGUE

Rainy day
Cul-de-sac
December cold
Mom and Pop cafe
Table in back
Old Jewish part of the city
Hoping this snack
Will inspire a Plan B

Mulled cider in a cup
My cap pulled down, my collar up
Like in that old war movie
The Sorrow And The Pity
A blind old cat named Moses
Twitches and dozes
By the antique register up front
And on the soapstone countertop
A silver menorah
That's survived the diaspora
The whole *mishpocha*
Making me feel guilty, inadequate, alone
It's Hanukkah
I should be home
I thumb the Fodors in my lap

This afternoon after a nap
In that half-a-star hostel
I adjourned to the over-worked urinal
Not even a minute
Someone stole my backpack
With my passport in it
And a copy of The Trial
(I know. How ironic!)
Hell!

Hell! Hell! Hell!
Trying not to panic
But I'm hopeless in Czech
How do you say *I require the authorities?*
This plate of pickled herring and latke
Colluding now with last night's vodka
I accuse Kafka and alcohol
Of inspiring this calamity

GOOD OLD AMERICAN BEER

Good old American beer
Makes the snakecharmer fumble his flute.
Lit, Krishna whispers in his ear,

"There's nothing to fear!
Let King Cobra lick your foot!"
Good old American beer

Makes boundaries disappear
And allegiances become moot
Mother Mary nibbles on Mohammed's ear

In a seedy hotel in old Tangier
Wearing nought but her birthday suit
Good old American beer

Slaps a grin on Dull Despair
Waters the old Cosmic Root,
Conducts a choir in the world's cupped ear

Led by morning's chanticleer
And midnight's moaning prostitute
Good old American beer
Makes God's mysterious intentions clear

TORNADO ALLEY

"In this part of creation
There's an on-going conversation
Between people and the sky

If you're smart
You take part
Trusting your gut
More than your eye

A wetted finger
Doppler radar, those
Will tell you where the wind blows
But it takes a subtler antenna
To detect the wind's agenda
Before everything goes quiet
And the barn swallows that were just there
Disappear—abracadabra—
Into the purple air
And a scary calm ensues

Like when your old man used to
Suddenly fill the doorway of your room
Pissed, pie-eyed
Belt in hand
That numb expression
The mask of doom
His jaw set that certain way
You knew' you weren't gonna like
What he had to say
Or was about to do
Nor ever understand
The reason for the reprimand

This is how the wise sons of the prairie know
(Well aware before interrupted radio
Or air-horn's blare)
Of the coming mindless blow

At night of course in these environs
You just pray to God and listen for the sirens

PEACE ON EARTH

inspired by a visit to the Johnson County Fair.

We, enlightened, snigger at these pageants
      in which nubile girls parade,
prim in swimsuits and sashes, color-coded,
      before panels of politicos, local celebrities,
self-medicating cosmetologists,
      to vie for scholarships, modeling contracts
but most importantly just the chance
      to be a Pickle Queen, or Miss
Junior Johnson County for a year—

We, enthralled, engender in our daughters
      an appetite for plaudits that require of them
a scrutiny like buzzards circling a potential meal
      with all attendant chagrin,
so they might be acknowledged most attractive, most
      congenial, or at least among the most—

We, Americans, who so deplore (constitutionally!)
      the precepts of monarchy and privilege
so readily embrace them in the tyranny of our dreams
      and long there to be set apart by nature as
"most enlightened", "most beautiful", "most beloved of God"—

Is it not the same? Is it not just one dream
      in which we snigger and are enthralled and stand up
as Americans, hand over heart, holding our breath,
      because the waxing Master
of Ceremonies has just asked our timorous daughter
      "If you could give the world one gift,
what would it be?"

MARQUIS OF QUEENSBERRY, REVISED

The man whose back is against a wall—
let none forbid him
bite and claw, or butt like a billygoat
to extricate his punished body
from its perilous state.

Adrenal surge exempts him
from the cheeky niceties of Christ;
its trumping mandate trumpeting
"Survive, persist!"

No self-respecting pug
should ever shoulder
inequities like Job.
Backed into a corner, his job
is bob and jab, deliver pain,
 not just stand and suffer.

*

The pilgrim who opts to wander deep
into the desert to tempt real thirst
will never be disappointed.
He will also be anointed
a dope of the highest order.
Because wisdom never wanders far from water.

To take the measure of your soul, my son,
summon the devil by offering sport
on a field, in theory, level
but actually undulate, unpredictable
chopped as the great, moody sea.

Toss toe to toe with perdition,
endure eye-gouges, low blows, lacing,
and the mendacity of a referee, who
(knowing who butters his bread)
turns a blind eye to merciless proceedings.

No doctor or judge to stop the bout.
No cornerman to throw the towel in.
You're on your own till the end of *anything goes*,
which is when the last gasping light goes out.

TWO SIGNS
for Carrie

1- LOVELESS MACHINE & GRINDING (A VALENTINE)

LOVELESS MACHINE & GRINDING is
the name of a tool-and-die business.

Driving past I saw their sign
on my way to buy Valentine

flowers for a woman I want to impress
with solicitude and tenderness.

The fact that she's young and beautiful
has spurred me to be more dutiful

than I usually am.
Her blue eyes like an anthem,

convinced me with one glance,
to fix bayonet and advance

(forgive the martial metaphor-ing).
In the marketplace of love, ignoring

the demands of carnality
requires huge supplies of venality,

forkings and crossings, even summoning the Devil's hand
to pardon the soul for the body's command.

So what if the roses I bestow
are an unequivocal *quid pro quo?*

My flowers for hers does not defame
the beauty of flowers nor her good name.

Like a sign myself if my message is sincere,
Old Scratch will have no leverage here.

So, *LOVELESS MACHINE & GRINDING* sign,
inspire me more! Shall I also offer wine

to warm and redden those supple lips
that I might test them with little nips

of teeth and tongue? Then (to honor her soul)
Open wide! Devour her whole!

Flowers and wine. Yes! Now let poetry
be the tipping gift to smooth entry

into her secret Eden
as lush as before Christ's pardon)

God knows words are tools
as apt for breaking as making rules.

The *LOVELESS MACHINE & GRINDING* sign cried
out for its truth to be verified:

that love leaves everything to death, its heir.
That love abides in poetry. That poetry is everywhere!

2- MISREADING: A SONG

CHINA CASTANETS 4 SALE!
says the plywood sign
sloppily lettered in red paint
fixed to an elm with one nail.

A roadside elm, in demise.
The nail, 10 penny, a ridiculous size,
as if the deal were so urgent
there was no time to improvise

better schemes to publish word of it:
this unprecedented chance
to acquire an instrument so exotic
I, for one, never heard of it.

A hybrid, it seems, of traditions so
distinct they stand for opposition.
Outcast offspring of East and West!
Lorca dancing with Li-Po!

Am I the only one intrigued
enough to turn around and
take the rutted driveway down
to where a barn, fatigued

from years of bearing heavy snows
stands, sway-backed, lurching
toward a farmhouse whose only creature
comfort is a border of lilies and willows

and knock, curious to know who'd be
purveying such arcana? Is
no one else enamored of weird marriages?
The Buddhist Inquisition? Flamenco tai chi?

Behind the porch screen, the careworn
face of an old woman appears,
pale as a daytime moon, wondering
what supplicant would use a car's horn

to conjure her from her kitchen. Alarmed,
she latches the door, squints through the screen
perplexed by my inquiry.
"Mister, you sure are mis-informed."

"We sell tomatoes, cukes and corn.
Our roadside stand's a half mile yonder.
You mean them china *cabinets*?
As advertised, they're out in the barn,"

Delight is where you find it.
The road offers many signs
whose deep value consists in
misreading. I don't mind it,

my disappointment. Difference
always blossoms. —That flower is God's blessing:
Tonight I'll savor homegrown tomatoes
and the silence of China castanets.

THE SECRET LIFE OF NUMBERS

My fourth grade teacher, Polly Perkins, asks
"Now Adam, do you like pie?"
I sense a trap like fly-paper glue, but I answer:
"Yes Ma'am, my Grandma's rhubarb pie, I do."

"Now would you rather have a *third* or a *fourth*
of your Grandma's yummy pie?"
Fully baited, I demur,
look to my fingers
while the wiser kids purr
like cats set to pounce, their narrowed eyes
forecasting my ignominious demise.

So it was in 1959 my own
diminishment taught me fractions,
and how to survive as
the smallest of the small.
"The beauty of numbers," Miss Perkins said,
"is that they'll never lie."
My Grandma died in 1973,
went with God to Infinity.
I remember her pie.

From A CHILD'S GARDEN OF ANTI-PSYCHOTICS
with respect and apologies to Robert Louis Stevenson

Oh how I like to go up on a drug,
Up on a drug when I'm down!

I do think it the pleasantest way
To conjure a smile from a frown!

How better to placate my tantrum, my tizzy
Or vacate my mind when my mind is too busy?

Or shush the weird confidantes here in my head
When they start recommending I'm better off dead.

Unloved is the child who's always upset
So give me my apple juice and caplet

Of clozapine, lexipro, sweet adderall
To slow my ascent and cushion my fall

Poor Mommy and Daddy! What else can they do?
Shrinks have convinced them their options are few

Pharmaceuticals by far the likeliest way
To divert my career as the moon's protégé

And keep me within their familial embrace
Though dimmer in eye and slacker in face

BAD STUDENT

Oh, sensei
You say
"Inhabit the moment!
All else is illusion!"
But how?

As soon as it's now
It's then before I
Can empty my mind
Prop open the door
To let the now in.

Evanescence by a nose
Beats incandescence
Every time. Yes, I'm awake
But incarnate, uncouth.
And maybe not meant for Ultimate Truth

Though the Zen stick still hurts when it smacks me,
Mercifully, only momentarily

DELICACY

Eeka! Eeka!
No more the sleepy seaside town
Shiminoseki, Japan

Eeka! Eeka!
Fishmarket seismic with commerce
Louder more feral
Than the Nikkei Stock Exchange

Eeka! Eeka!
Bidding for fuku
The infamous poison pufferfish
That legendary delicacy
Whose liver alone contains
Enough tetrodotoxin
To kill five hearty men

Suddenly the floor goes silent when
An agent for an unnamed billionaire
Steps up to the market auctioneer and
Slips a soft hand, pale
And cool as beluga roe
Up the ample sleeve of his snow-white jacket
There, obscured from public view,
Subtle pinchings of fey fingers
On a muscled forearm convey
How many thousands the mystery client
Is willing to pay for
The choicest fuku of this particular day

Dr. Englebert Kaempfer, a German missionary
Posted to Nagasaki in 1690
Described fuku as "preferred devices"
For anguished wives of sailors lost at sea
To rejoin their spouses

In journals of his second voyage, 1774,
Captain James Cook mentions *fuku*
A curious gift from the Kanak of New Caledonia
Taken aboard *The Resolution*, rendered
Meticulously for the naturalist's catalogue
In sepia ink, then disposed of
Unceremoniously because of its "unholy stink"
Fed to a hungry ship-board pig that forthwith coughed
turned up its toes and died performing a contorted jig

Mitsuguru Banda
Eighth in a line of famous Kabuki dancers
Declared a "national treasure "in 1974
Declared dead in a restaurant in '75
Having eaten four portions of fuku liver
Declaring it "out of this world"
Before pitching forward into his plate
Like a reckless cliff diver

Properly
the delicacy
Is elegantly arranged
On painted porcelain plates
Served paper thin
Translucent strips
Masterfully cut to resemble
Chrysanthemum petals, peacocks, Mt. Fuji
Carefully prepared they say
Fuku is safe to consume
But more die from it each year
Than from mistaking the poison mushroom

For the timid may I recommend instead
From seaside gift shops lanterns made
From the bodies of fuku specially preserved
Or perhaps an expensive wallet composed
Of the buff of its ventral skin
For the timid, harmless curios

For those who'd risk
The delicacy of pufferfish
Fate determines the price
It's vulgar in the etiquette of gods
To concern oneself with dying or the odds
Of it while dining at their table
All grace is in experience and
The taste of death, not trying

THE NEW CIVIL DEFENSE

Old school taught us duck and cover
Don't peek out until it's over

Build a shelter underground
Periscope to snoop around

See what's transpiring up above
And, since push might come to shove,

Good to have a loaded gun
To discourage anyone

Of one's less prepared neighbors
From leeching off one's prescient labors

Stocked canned goods, water for a month
At least to give the sickened earth

A chance to purge, regurgitate
De-toxify and re-create

Cool down and breathe enough to lend
Itself to mother us again

Those unfortunates near ground-zero
Will be rendered into shadow

Silhouettes upon a wall
(If anything still stands at all)

Those who survive the blast, no doubt
Will be dusted by fallout

And suffer very horribly
(e.g. Hiroshima, Nagasaki)

The old atomic *que sera,*
Predicts a jungle-y kind of law

So what progress have we made
Since I was back in second grade

Cowering beneath my little desk
Expecting my face to deliquesce?

Bigger bombs, more paranoic fuss
To more efficiently destroy us

Guess that's just the way it goes
Plus ca change, plus ca la meme chose

New children in the same environs
Terrified of air-raid sirens

Same old God, same old Devil
No defense is ever civil

A SESTINA SEARCHING FOR MARTIN LEVINE

Martin Levine's in Rhode Island.
But you can't find him there.
In that smallest of states he does business
Beneath umbrellas of imaginative names
Like *Invisible Melvin* or *Levi the Duck.*
No bigger name in the world of music

Than *Martin Levine*, says Martin Levine. Who in music
Wouldn't kill to land
A big fat recording contract
With a well-regarded label? "I can help you there,"
Said Martin Levine, "I have names."
But why so many? I guess that's none of my business.

Singer/songwriter, that's my business.
I've been showcasing my music
For years in bars with names
Like *Starlight Lounge,* and *Sweet Pete's* out on Long Island,
Honing my craft there
In dives where one learns quickly to duck

Beer bottles, insults and marriage proposals, and conduct
Oneself like a professional in a business
That rarely rewards the meek-at-heart. There,
In the *Starlight*, by mere chance Martin Levine heard my music
On his way home from the airport after an island
Vacation in the Caribbean, one of those islands named,

Vincent, John, or *Thomas*, saints' names,
Evidence of the Church's reach and conduct
In the New World, tucking island after island
Into the fold of Rome's wallet. Sharp business!
Transposing native drums for sacred music;
Seducing (with a Virgin!) the voodoo deities pre-dominant there.

Martin whispered his private number in my ear.
Slipped me cards full of contacts—names
Of agents, producers. Said my music took his breath away, my music
Guaranteed *Cristal* in my future instead of *Cold Duck!*
Said we'd re-define the music business
As soon as he got back from Rhode Island.

Searching for names in Rhode Island, residential and business,
You'll first get a tape of dull music, then directory assistance to instruct,
Regretfully, no listing for *Levi the Duck.*

I don't blame the conduct of music or the multiplicity of names.
Truth's always a tricky business. It will remain to be seen
If the truth of little Rhode Island can contain one Martin Levine.

X AND THE ASTERISK

X stands for what you don't know.
The devil's crossroads. A warped crucifix.
The tiny asterisk says "See below".

Gentle direction simple to follow
Like a snowflake's charming lisp.
X demands you bow

To the *quid pro quo*
Tyranny of mathematics.
The tiny asterisk whispers "Just see below

For affirmation of what is so."
Beware the basilisk
Of X. What you don't know

Can hit you like a hammer blow
From behind. But that little star, brave aviatrix,
The radiant asterisk coos "See below.

Clouds are breaking! There! An archipelago!
A place to land! A face to kiss!
And poor old X will never know."
So heed the tiny asterisk. Just see below. *

THE ART OF JOY
for Carrie and Mac, her new puppy

We're all on a leash of some kind
Time Space Life Death
All at the mercy of kindness and cruelty
A dog's life for sure
Strange new worlds unrolling every day
A voice to look up to
With a tilt of our head
Trying to understand
What it wants us to do

www.ingramcontent.com/pod-product-compliance
Lightning Source LLC
LaVergne TN
LVHW051609080426
835510LV00020B/3203